TRANSITION TO RETIREMENT
The Uncharted Course

Carol Baird-Krul and Enise Olding

Pacific Edge Publishing Ltd.

Acknowledgements
We acknowledge the financial support of the Government of Canada
through the Book Publishing Industry Development Program (BPIDP)
and the British Columbia Book Publishing Tax Credit for our publishing
activities.

Library and Archives Canada Cataloguing in Publication

Baird-Krul, Carol
    Transition to retirement : the uncharted course / Carol Baird-Krul,
    Enise Olding.

ISBN 1-894948-05-X

    1. Retirement. 2. Self-actualization (Psychology). 3. Retirement–
    Psychological aspects. 4. Retirees–Life skills guides. I. Olding, Enise
    II. Title.

HQ1062.B33 2006   646.7'9   C2006-905847-4

Pacific Edge Publishing Ltd.
1773 El Verano Drive
Gabriola, B.C.
Canada V0R 1X6
Telephone: 1-800-668-8806
Fax: 1-800-956-8299
email: info@PacificEdgePublishing.com
website: www.PacificEdgePublishing.com

Photos © 2006 John van den Hengel

Printed and bound in Canada

DEDICATION

This book is dedicated to DRA, a partnership which gave us the key to open the door to a whole new world of possibilities, personal growth and achievement, and provided an opportunity for us to be of service to that dynamic demographic fondly referred to as the Boomers.

ACKNOWLEDGEMENTS

A book cannot be written without the help of many people who along the way advise, suggest and inspire. We would like to recognize and express our appreciation for support and encouragement to all those who have hosted, attended or been featured in our workshop *Transition to Retirement: The Uncharted Course.* Particular thanks go to Joan Berrey and Muriel Reiber for reading our completed manuscript, and also to Diana Mumford and Ron Mumford of Pacific Edge Publishing Ltd. for believing in us. Special thanks go to our closest family members: John, Karen, Julia, Kees, Janet and Liam. And last but not least, many thanks to all those who have listened, discussed, explored and debated the topic of retirement with us.

CONTENTS

INTRODUCTION

Planning for retirement isn't only about finances and unlimited free time as we discovered when we retired. After a satisfying career in education, Carol had, or so she thought, carefully prepared for retirement and life beyond; while for Enise, retirement suddenly arrived when she was informed that her administrative job was being eliminated immediately.

As friends and keen west coast boaters, whenever we got together we discussed life and the future, and soon realized that we were both experiencing a similar sense of loss and lack of focus. Wanting to understand this unexpected turmoil of emotions and disorientation, we set out to find some answers. Typical of information-hungry baby boomers, we searched for resources covering the psychological and emotional aspects of transitioning from work to retirement, but found very few.

Eventually, we were prompted to fill this lack by combining a myriad of professional skills that include marketing, teaching, administration, management and international employment placement, with our own retirement experiences. This decision resulted in the creation, development and presentation of a series of workshops on the topic of transitioning from work to retirement that we designed for those contemplating retirement, for those already retired and for others who are wanting to get started on a new venture, but just don't know where to start.

The workshops, *Transition to Retirement: The Uncharted Course* ©, *Recently Retired: Charting a New Course* © and *Ideas ... Enhanced and Advanced* © have been presented at universities, school districts, financial institutions and also in private groups, health and wellness committees, and to individuals. As well, we are regular contributors to national and local publications, and appear as guest speakers.

Over time, requests for information on the subject encouraged us to create this book as a "heads up" for others entering retirement. It covers the unexpected aspects of the transition from work to retirement; exploring attitudes, assumptions and myths, and focusing on psychological and emotional planning. Combining research, survey responses and aspects of our own journeys, we offer insights into what might be expected by those contemplating their own transition into retirement, and provide a variety of tools with which to smooth the passage.

We continue to learn from our new venture—retirement—and look forward to exploring this most interesting stage of life and sharing our discoveries with others.

CHAPTER 1

DESTINATION RETIREMENT
The Voyage from Here to There

One day you are at work, the next day you are retired. What might you expect to be feeling—joy,
relief, a sense of loss, boredom, a lack of structure
in your life? On the outside it might appear that
you're enjoying cruising along in your newfound
freedom, but inside you are likely to be experiencing some unsettling moments, especially as
time goes on.

Prepare to Plan

Transition from work to retirement requires
preparation and planning. Much valuable and
necessary information is available about important issues such as financial planning, including
pension and investment options, and lifestyle decisions such as where to live, how to live and whether

or not to travel. However, often overlooked in these preparations is the need for psychological and emotional planning. Many are fearful of the mere thought of retiring and simply don't want to take a close look at where life has led them and where it might take them now, preferring instead to deal only with more concrete items such as money and lifestyle.

Although it is inevitable, most people entering retirement are not expecting to review a lifetime of experiences, values, assertions and perceptions. Along with everything else there is to think about, this particular aspect is not easy to contemplate and often makes for a less than smooth passage. And thoughts of retirement are often linked with thoughts of old age—definitely not a particularly appealing combination. Being aware of this beforehand helps normalize what could otherwise be a disturbing and unsettling period of life.

Most people spend more time planning their annual vacations than their retirement.

Finding things to keep busy may very well not be enough for today's retirees who want to continue to feel significant, contributory and valued. Taking a look at perceptions and expectations about retirement and aging is a good first step towards making a positive, interesting and enlightened transition from work to retirement.

No matter what course you are planning, the voyage into retirement will take you into uncharted waters and through all types of weather. There is much work and reflection to do before you are feeling comfortable and fully engaged in the prospect of retirement. The markers in this book will help you steer a course towards your destination.

Aids to Navigation

- Take time—really take the time to think about your own retirement.

- Beware of imposing a stereotypical version of retirement upon yourself.

- Be realistic as you consider the options and limitations of your own retirement.

- Exchange fear for curiosity when you contemplate life as an older person.

- Finances aside, think about the biggest retirement challenges you think you'll have.

CHAPTER 2

DOCKSIDE
Retirement on the Horizon

Retirement comes in many ways—by reaching a certain age, corporate downsizing, health limitations, family demands or a financial windfall. It can be phased in, abrupt or drawn out; desired or feared; planned or unplanned. No matter which way it arrives, there is, as in all life passages, a period of adjustment from one stage in life to another.

Being one of the baby boomer generation reaching this important passage in life, you know that retirement is definitely the buzzword for today. As retirement approaches, you may be feeling a mixture of joy and trepidation, but just as you have always been quick to search for pertinent information and find workable solutions when life's challenges come your way, you will continue to seek out resources that available to create a new way of being in this next life stage.

Your generation, as it progressed through life, has reviewed the status quo and made changes to better suit your vision of society, community and yourselves. Poised now on the cusp of retirement, you will be looking back at previous retirement models and may wish to break out of some stereotypes and redefine what retirement is now.

When are you going to retire?

It's Not Just About the Money

Because finances play a hugely important part in preparing for retirement, there is a lot of help, information and resources readily available in bookstores, libraries and on the Internet. Calculators work overtime as this topic is delved into, dissected and the many options considered. While undoubtedly an important, and for some, an all-consuming part of the preparation, there is also the rarely discussed and often glossed over aspect of the emotional preparation for retirement.

As retirement beckons, there's that allure of freedom from schedules, having time to do what you want, when you want. But also, there are the often unbidden frissons of discomfort when limitations are considered: age, financial, physical, family and abilities. Questions and emotions that are often ignored in the days of preparation lurk ready to surface when the responsibilities of work have disappeared. How best can you make use of this preparatory period?

Take Time to Take Stock

Taking the time to thoughtfully consider and understand the transitional period is key to embarking on your journey towards a fulfilling and fully engaged retirement. This is the time frame from when you are no longer actively working at your job to when you become positively engaged in your new life as a retired person. Time for reflection now is extremely important, otherwise all kinds of stereotyped overlays can impose and hinder forward movement.

What is it about retirement that worries you? Excites you?

What we found, and what others in surveys confirm, is that there are four relatively distinct phases in the transition from work to reaching a fully engaged retirement. While there is no definite time limit for the transitional period, it generally lasts approximately 12 to 18 months, depending on the individual involved and their circumstances. Being well adjusted in the position of a retired person, no matter what retirement looks like, is the goal of all who make the decision to leave their primary career. So how do you get off to a good start?

We will look at the four phases by reviewing the specific characteristics of each, providing a variety of interesting and practical information, posing questions and pertinent comments pertaining to each particular phase, and finally providing

summaries to each phase called Aids to Navigation. These, together with a variety of real-life
experiences, and thought-provoking side-bar
comments, will be the tools to use to help the
transition be a positive one. If an informed start
to retirement life planning is what you're after,
then spending time to understand the overall
transitional period and the individual phases is
crucial.

Aids to Navigation

- Give equal time to emotional planning and financial planning as you begin to prepare for retirement.

- Successfully navigating the transitional phase from work to retirement means you have completed the first leg of the voyage.

- Remember that outmoded images of retirement don't apply to you.

- Read about the topics of retirement and aging.

- Remain flexible and open to changes in your plans.

- Look beyond the immediate promise of freedom from the constraints of the workplace.

- Remain curious and keep an open mind during the transition from work to retirement.

CHAPTER 3

STOWING THE GEAR
Getting Ready to Go

At work it is fairly easy to figure out where someone stands in the overall scheme of things. We
instinctively recognize our equals, those we can
bypass and those to whom attention needs to
be paid. Some have business cards or signs on
their office doors, vehicles or elsewhere indicat-
ing their roles within the organization. Over the
years people have moved up or down the scale of
importance or influence, and some have moved
on. Things have changed, sometimes for the better and sometimes not. Likely you are aware of
the history and environment of your workplace,
and it all feels fairly familiar. There are routines
and expectations at work that become a part of
your life. But, who are YOU outside of your job,

profession, occupation, place of work and what you do there?

Hello my Name is ...

Try taking the ten-second test.

Scenario: You are retired, and you meet someone in a social setting for the first time. The situation requires that you introduce yourself and provide some information to the other person.

What will you miss when you leave your job? Why?

Task: Take a few moments to think of, or find a piece of paper and pen to jot down, your response as to how you will introduce yourself without any reference to your job, title, type of work you did, place of work or previous employers.

You have ten seconds – GO!

Now, consider the task you have just completed. Did you run out of space or hardly write a word? Was it difficult or easy to think of yourself as someone outside of your current job? What do you think about what you have written? Is it interesting and do you sound interesting? Or does it seem insipid, vague, boring, lacking in direction or focus?

Sometimes those who find it easy to define themselves are so anxious to leave work that finding non-work oriented descriptors is not difficult. Others have developed well-rounded lives that provide them with a feeling of significance whether at work or outside of it. On the other hand, some people find it difficult to come up with interesting and satisfying descriptions of themselves without a reference to their job. In those cases, some long and hard thinking and planning should be taking place well before retirement to consider what can provide the same level of satisfaction and pride that is found at work.

What won't you miss when you leave your job? Why?

Either way, mentally casting aside the many years of effort and contribution you have given to your job is not what should be done. Rather, no matter what emotions are generated by your prospective retirement, honouring your past contribution to your workplace is essential because you have, over the years, given a lot of yourself, your time and energy to your job.

When in transition from your primary career to a balanced and engaged life in retirement, an evaluation of those years at work is very helpful. This evaluation needs to take place over a period of time and not necessarily while still employed. Viewing past work contributions, trials, triumphs and tribulations with more objectivity from a distance of time helps put the work experience into perspective. It is important to contemplate who YOU are beyond who you are, or were, in your workplace.

Really Retiring

Talking about retirement in an abstract way, often with a financial focus, protects people from actually having to visualize what it might be like on the day-to-day level. Despite the fact that they are going through the motions of preparing to leave work, retirement is still a vague notion that is "out there somewhere" but definitely not here, and not now. If retirement arrives sooner than expected, then it becomes up close and personal in a way that is truly startling. Even if the process of retirement evolves in the way in which it has been planned, there is a moment when the reality of the situation hits home—no more job, no more benefits, no name tag, no business card, no longer on the email list, no more voicemail and no longer a representative of that organization, no schedule. You become a free agent in life, a situation that can be both exhilarating and yet tumultuously devastating.

Whether it is loved or despised, the workplace took up a lot of space in your life. Work related thoughts, anxieties, worries, pleasures, challenges, triumphs, participation, teamwork, comradeship, and common goals imposed on everyday life. When holidays were taken, how a sick colleague would impact your day, precious weekends, and time off regulated your social activities and dictated how life would be structured. Then it is all *gone*.

How many titles or job descriptions have you had?

Leaving with regret or delight is still leaving, and it still means no longer being a part of that group of people or organization. Turning away from life as you knew it is to experience a loss, while turning around and facing the future as a retired person, an older person, is to embark upon a journey into the unknown.

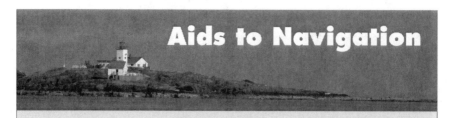

Aids to Navigation

- Think about who you are outside of your work title or designation.

- Consider how you might present yourself once you leave work.

- Recall for future use the coping skills used in the past when major changes occurred in your life.

- The transition from work to retirement requires planning and thought, so take your time.

- Take a look at perceptions and expectations about retirement and aging as a good first step in your planning.

- Consider whether you will want to change your appearance once you leave work, and why.

- Imagine the type of lifestyle you want when you first retire, and later.

CHAPTER 4

CASTING OFF
Retirement Past and Present

Retirement—when you hear or see that word what do you think, how do you feel, what image comes to mind?

You are not alone if you come up with phrases like:

Free time	No pressure
Freedom	No schedules

Many people who are contemplating retirement look forward to a future in which they can please themselves and don't have to march to other people's drums.

Now, what happens when you think about the word *senior*—are your thoughts and ideas equally positive?

Or do you notice yourself responding less enthusiastically with words like:

Old	Illness
Discounts	Poverty

Again, you would not be alone because while the word *retirement* has generally positive connotations, the word *senior* has mainly negative ones.

Words and Meanings

Apply the word "retired" to you, what comes to mind?

It's worth taking a look at the words *retirement* and *senior* because we will be hearing them pretty much constantly for the rest of our lives. Both words engender stereotypical responses that have little to do with their actual meanings. Most dictionaries state that the word *retirement* originally comes from the old French word "tirer" that means to take back or withdraw. In English, by adding the prefix "re" we have the word *retire* with all its unspoken connotations.

Interestingly, the meaning of the word *senior* is "one who is older or higher in rank." This is a considerably more positive definition than most people would expect. Perhaps if we were to use these two dictionary meanings rather than the stereotypical hidden ones that we have generally adopted, we would look upon this stage of life more favourably.

No matter how you think of yourself at this time of life—boomer, senior, retiree, middle-aged or mature, others might have different opinions.

This can be disconcerting as Carol found out shortly after she retired.

> *I travel regularly on a small ferry in British Columbia and everyone gets to know each other over a period of time. So it wasn't surprising that many passengers and crew knew when I retired from teaching. One day I was purchasing a ferry ticket and was told by the ticket seller that I didn't need to purchase a ticket that day. Puzzled, I asked, "Why?" The response, "Well, it's a Seniors' travel day—you're a senior, aren't you? You've retired."*

> *While some people might think it's great to get discounts because they have reached a certain age, for me it was not a happy moment when I realized that some people considered me a senior simply because I was retired! My definition of retired was someone who was vibrant, active and involved in the world, while my definition of senior thrust my mind to dwelling on images of my grandparents' later lives.*

On the other hand, that senior label is bestowed by various organizations on people 50 years and up, and if that coincides with something that benefits you, it makes the label a little easier to wear, as Enise discovered.

> *When I realized I could attend our community centre gym, swimming pool and weight training room for a discounted price because I hap-*

pened to be 55 years old, I thought it was excellent. I've known people to refuse such discounts because they didn't want others to think of them as being seniors. But I think the young person in the ticket office would consider me a senior whether I thought I was or not! It's something I have to get used to about myself now.

When is a senior not a senior?

When it's applied to you, of course! You pick up the paper and there you are, well, not you personally but you collectively as a senior. Overnight you've been designated from a respected, knowledgeable, influential and vital member of the workforce to a societal group known as seniors. And as such you might be depicted as a kickboxing grandma, sought as a likely candidate for a variety of mobility assistance gadgets, nudged into making a choice for final arrangements, invited to join a motorcycle club or to consider a change of lifestyle. You and your parents weren't adolescents, teenagers or middle-aged together, but now in retirement you are lumped together and categorized as seniors.

Apply the word "senior" to you, what comes to mind?

Whose idea was it, anyway?

Today, retirement is something most people in the developed world consider to be a normal progression or phase in their lives. In fact, it is a relatively recent social development. Up until the early 20th century, work was considered an integral and necessary part of life and most people did it until they died or were physically incapable of continuing. Families supported those who could not work. The social safety net and phenomenon that we know as Pensions and Retirement, was instituted in the late 19th Century. It is commonly agreed that around 1881, William the First of Germany suggested that his government adopt a policy of retirement from work with a pension. The Chancellor of the day, Otto Von Bismarck, complied and a pension for all working people was established. Originally the age for retirement from work was set at 70 but was later changed to 65, and this is now generally accepted as the retirement age. Today however, mandatory retirement is being challenged in a variety of workplaces, while retirement itself is being revamped, reorganized and rethought.

What do you consider a fulfilling retirement to be?

Looking for a Role Model

Think of your grandparents or parents and consider what their retirements looked like to you. And all those stereotypical retirement images you've seen over the years—do they reflect what you envision for yourself? Probably not—sitting in the proverbial rocking chair and watching the world go by is rarely an option considered by those currently contemplating retirement.

Certainly there are those who, because they haven't thought about what life will be like after leaving work, react to actually being retired much like a "deer caught in the headlights"—bemused, a little stunned, disoriented and lost. Happily today there's a new type of retiree—productive, involved, and energetic and not about to settle for being anything less. These are people who do not consider themselves old at 65, and after retiring from their primary career have moved on to another exciting career. And that career can be a myriad of things—a business, a new occupation, a volunteer position, or indulging in a particular passion to the max.

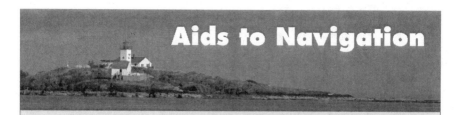

Aids to Navigation

- Use your past experience—it is yours to use with wisdom now.

- Become well informed about the issues of aging.

- Feel free to redefine the image that both society and you have of retirement.

- If you don't like commonly used words that are assigned to you as an older person, think of some better ones and use them instead.

- Research and understand the aging process, find out why nature designed things this way.

- Think about what age is "old" and upon what have you based your belief.

CHAPTER 5

ON BOARD
The Journey Begins

The journey to retirement begins a lot earlier than you might expect. It might start when a colleague or a friend is retiring and it suddenly dawns on you that this will actually be happening to you as well, in the not so distant future. Or it might begin when the organization you work for undergoes a reorganization of some kind. Or maybe you have been eyeing the prospect of retirement for quite a few years and can hardly wait for the day to arrive. This first flirtation with the idea of our own retirement is often unsettling, and can become buried in the background of our lives, only to make itself known with more persistence as we encounter little reminders of this pending state.

Flirting with Retirement

To provide an example of the dawning awareness of retirement, we'd like to share with you an experience we offer during our workshops where we ask for two volunteers to "retire" instantly. This always causes great hilarity, lots of meaningful looks, and encouragement for people to volunteer. There are always two good sports who offer themselves up as volunteers. They are asked to pick up everything they brought in with them and leave, now. They are given a "Happy Retirement" balloon-festooned gift bag and cheered out of the door. This always causes a little flurry of activity, comments and excitement. Outside, the two "retirees" are separated from each other and given a pre-set period of time to look through their going away gift bags with a view to sharing their reactions with the rest of the group later. Meanwhile, back in the classroom, the others are considering a sample of the retirement greeting cards available in card shops today, and to do so they move into smaller groups for discussion purposes.

Besides financial planning, what have you done to prepare for retirement?

Considering the Cards

You might flirt with the idea of your own retirement as you scan the displays of greeting cards to choose one for someone who is retiring. Doubtless these cards are purchased with the kindest and best of intentions, and also based on assumptions of how the giver thinks the recipient feels about their retirement. The cards run the gamut from depicting a gentle entering into a life of prolonged, muted blandness, to hilarity about doing nothing every day of the week. There are the old chestnuts about no more deadlines, endless golf or some such leisure activity, sad colleagues being left behind, a job well done, enjoying the fruits of your labour, being put out to pasture, getting on with real life, being a child again and so on. Stereotypes abound and often the retiree on the card is depicted as being greatly advanced in years, bringing yet another shock to the receiver. Being seen as an 80-pluser instead of a 50-pluser just because of the retirement tag can be rather upsetting for the recipients.

What type of retirement card might you choose for yourself?

As an example, a participant in one of our workshops was shaken by the starkness of an image on a card which featured an office desk upon which there was an IN basket and an OUT basket. The IN basket was overflowing with paper, and in the OUT basket sat a cartoon depiction of the retiree.

When people view the large selection of retirement cards we've gathered, there are always spirited discussions as to what they see now that they are looking at the cards with their own retirement in mind. Next time you're in a store that sells greeting cards, take a moment to have a close look at the ones celebrating retirement. Over the past two or three years the selection has increased and there are many more positive, current, modern and enlightened cards being offered that better reflect the lifestyle and image of current retirees.

How do you view retirement parties, celebrations or gatherings?

A Brush with Retirement

Now let's return to our workshop when the two volunteer retirees return to share their experiences with the others. Inevitably their original seats have been taken by others, so that some rearrangement has to go on to bring them back into the fold. Graciously, and often with much insight and humour, the volunteer retirees discuss the contents of their gift bags. These bags contain an assortment of items of topics typically considered appropriate for the retiree: golf pamphlet, pack of cards, notepad, pen, travel schedule, retirement home brochure, spa price list, best-selling novel. Sometimes people like to keep the entire contents of the bags and others don't want to keep anything, and some carefully consider each and every item and then decide which of them best reflects their vision of retirement. Interestingly, all of the workshop volunteer retirees to date say they found it difficult or uncomfortable to leave the class, even though in some cases they didn't really know the other participants personally, to go off on their own, only to come back and find after such a short time that their chairs had been taken or moved.

If you could choose, what type of send-off would you like when you leave your job for good?

Cards, gifts, celebrations, rites of passage, acknowledgements of the milestones in life are all fraught with difficulty, and especially so when the occasion happens to be marking a retirement of one of your colleagues presaging the occasion of your own departure.

We'd hasten to add that the above two exercises in our workshops are offered with warmth, humour, sincerity and generosity and in no way are participants compelled to participate beyond their own comfort level. Many participate to such a surprisingly enthusiastic extent that it's always a good time to take a break before launching into the nuts and bolts segment of Transition to Retirement which is the next aspect—The Continuum.

Aids to Navigation

- Look beyond media imposed stereotypical retirement images.

- Look beyond your own self-imposed stereotypical retirement images.

- Think about your life beyond the collegiality and familiarity of your workplace.

- Consider the lifestyles of your friends and colleagues who are retired: what are your observations?

- Check out the biographies of those who, in your opinion, are successful retirees.

- What do you think of the often used term "senior moment"?

CHAPTER 6

THE CONTINUUM
Discovering the Phases

What actually happens during the transition from work to an actively engaged retirement? A good question and one we pondered for some time. Eventually we realized that neither of us, nor any of the subsequently surveyed people we contacted during our research, nor any we read about, had experienced just one long, undiluted stretch of time immediately after retirement in which to sort out a new life.

Rather, the whole transitional period was made up of a series of phases. But unlike a general time line that starts at 0 and ends at 100, we found that the phases of adjustment and introspection that make up the transitional period did not go in a straight line. Instead the phases ebbed and flowed like the sea, crossing over and under each other as events triggered emotions and thoughts. Although throughout this process the phases themselves remained distinct and clearly identifiable, the turbulence of awakening awareness often obscured them. We call this series of phases The Continuum.

The more we thought about our own experiences and those of others, we determined that there seemed to be four distinct phases that a person encounters in the period between leaving work and being actively engaged in the retirement segment of life. We discovered that these phases collectively last anywhere from 12 to 18 months—some people passed through in a shorter period of time, while others took longer. We also found that some people spent a long period of time in particular phases while others sailed through with nary a thought. In other words, the transition from being on the job to being involved in a fulfilling and satisfying retirement is not the same for everyone. Nevertheless, no matter what the timeframe or the emotional experience, one way or another the four phases of The Continuum are experienced by every person who retires from work.

The Transitional Phases of The Continuum

Sunny With Cloudy Periods

This is a time when all is well and as a newly retired person you are basking in the euphoria of no work commitments or responsibilities.

Stormy Weather

Just as bad weather often follows calm and balmy days, this is a time of tossing and turning within your psyche as you sort out who you are and how you want the rest of your life to be.

Safe Harbour

This phase of The Continuum is a peaceful, introspective time when you might explore your innermost thoughts, feelings and desires in a safe place. Once this phase is passed, you enter into the final phase of the transitional period.

Charting Your Own Course

This is a time when you begin to look forward rather than backwards, outwards instead of inwards. A time when you can truly start to "Chart Your Own Course," deciding what will actively and holistically engage you in this new segment of your life called retirement.

Not Simply a Passing Phase

Although we refer to the phases separately and each has its own distinct characteristics, keep in mind that these phases do not start and stop within certain periods of time. Even when the skies are clear and the winds fair, a storm can be brewing on the horizon. Just as in a storm, you will seek a calm, safe harbour to rest and consider where to head next. The Continuum helps to clarify and define this transitional process.

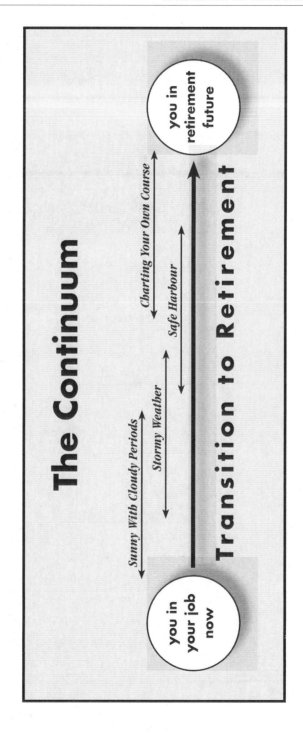

The Continuum

you in retirement future

Charting Your Own Course

Safe Harbour

Stormy Weather

Sunny With Cloudy Periods

you in your job now

Transition to Retirement

CHAPTER 7

SUNNY WITH CLOUDY PERIODS
The Early Days of Retirement

Whether retirement is far in the distance or in the relatively near future, each person plans their retirement with varying degrees of care, thought and awareness. However, regardless of the preparation or lack thereof, whether greeted with joy or trepidation, when retirement really does happen it is a wonderfully freeing time. The parties, the gifts, the good wishes highlight the heady thought that we are leaving for what we believe will be a liberating, exciting life of freedom after years of responsibility and regulations. The euphoria alone is enough to carry a person forward for some time, and for a while, retired life is everything that was expected—an extended high when time doesn't matter because there is lots of it. It's as though you are walking around in a bubble where everyday cares don't exist and the joy of waking up in the morning without having to go to work never gives any indication of dissipating. There are no rules, except the ones you want to impose on yourself, such as when to have coffee, when to read, when to do all the things you ever wanted to do. It's like being on vacation.

How do you imagine your first day of retirement will be?

The beginning days of retirement were every bit as wonderful as Carol had thought they would be.

I had thought very carefully about my retirement, and my family situation was such that when I was offered a buyout it all seemed to fit together so that everyone, including me, would be happy. I had the requisite going away parties and gifts. It all seemed to be wonderful and I looked forward to the freedom I saw beckoning enticingly when I actually left work on that last day. It seemed as though life was going to be a summer without end, a time to fill my life with all the enjoyable activities I'd been putting off because I didn't have the time or the energy while at work. The sun seemed brighter, my shoulders less tense and my step lighter when I got up each morning. So I never imagined that having the delicious dilemma of choosing one activity over another could become a problem.

Curling up with a good murder mystery is something I had always enjoyed as a way to relax, and I loved to dawdle over coffee and the newspaper on Sunday morning without a care as to the time. While working, I had wanted to but never seemed to have enough time to pick up my sketchbook. Yet when I had all the time in the world to indulge myself in these ways, I began to notice that the activities I had previously used as de-stressors no longer had the same appeal.

Be Careful What You Wish For

Whatever it is you love to do—sketch, garden, golf, walk, sew, carve—there's a good chance the activity will become less satisfying when done on a 24/7 basis. Once that joy or passion is not providing balance to the stress of your work life, it may lose some of its lustre. You've probably heard people approaching retirement joyously declare they won't be bored, they will golf (or whatever) every day! It's nice to indulge in the thought that doing something you love every day is possible, but reality shows that it may eventually become a tad boring.

What are you most looking forward to when you retire?

In the early days of retirement it seems highly unlikely and somewhat odd that any sense of unrest could possibly creep in and threaten to burst the bubble. Yet stirrings of discontent impinge with increasing frequency as the joy of being retired and freedom from the workaday worries gives way to a disquieting awareness that your life may not be all you thought it would be when you retired.

Unequal Farewells

Unlike Carol, many people leave work under less than cheerful circumstances. Some will become retired due to ill health, the need to take care of others, corporate re-organizations, amalgamations, downsizing or any number of reasons over which we have no control. Farewell events in these situations become fraught with difficulty when others are trying to honour a colleague yet be sympathetic, encouraging and cheerful. After all, is this person really retiring or just leaving work under unhappy circumstances?

If you could choose, what would your work leaving be like?

If this reflects your situation, when you meet former colleagues who are still working, you'll likely chat about your old workplace. Asserting that it is good to be "out of it" and indulging in life the way you want it, you will go your separate ways. Without doubt you'll be comparing working life with your life now as a retired person. Perhaps you will be overwhelmed with relief that you are not at the workplace any more, or perhaps there will be the sadness of no longer being part of the group. It can be awkward to meet former colleagues, as Enise found out.

Why are there parties and celebrations when someone retires?

> *Because my job was suddenly eliminated and I left the workplace within the space of a few days, it was awkward meeting former colleagues. But once they started talking about the workplace problems and issues, I realized how relieved I was not to still be a part of it. A weight had*

been lifted from my shoulders, and it was the first inkling I had that I was on the threshold of a more exciting life.

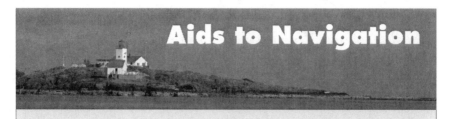

Aids to Navigation

- Enjoy the euphoria and holiday feeling, but be aware it won't last.

- Consider what you will do when your favourite recreational pursuits become ho-hum.

- What else does the world and your community have to offer?

- Think of the many options available to help you keep physically and mentally active.

- If you're living early retirement as though you are "on holiday," consider how your eating, sleeping and exercising habits might be changing.

- The early days of retirement can be full, busy and packed with action and experiences, but be aware that you might actually be taking on more stress under the guise of "fun and freedom."

Chapter 8

STORMY WEATHER
Discovering the Unexpected, and Yourself

No doubt about it, this is an uncomfortable place to be. It doesn't take much imagination to picture a raging storm with heavy winds, ominous dark clouds and drenching rain. Whether you are out in the elements or gazing through the window at nature's fury from the safety of your own home, one thing is certain—you tend to be wary and pay attention to what's going on. These are uncertain times when life and all its emotions hit you in the face as Enise discovered during her own sojourn in stormy weather.

> *After coasting along in the early days of retire-*
> *ment, when it felt marvellous to set my own*
> *timetable and indulge in my favourite leisure*
> *activities, it was quite a shock to find myself*

standing in my living room, repeating out loud, "What! What? What!" Questions and feelings that I had been avoiding over the last few weeks suddenly leapt forth and I had to take notice and acknowledge them.

What am I doing? What can I do? What a waste of my abilities! What a waste of precious time! What's wrong with me? What's happening, and why do I feel so unsettled, sad, angry and scared? I couldn't comprehend why I was complaining; after all I had wanted to be free of regular work hours and commitments. And, good heavens, I was after all actually past middle age; yet I was really fearful of being on that slippery slope into old age! Truth be told, I would not swap my new-found freedom for anything, and I didn't want to be back in the job I'd left, or any other for that matter. However, I couldn't understand why I didn't feel as joyous and exuberant as I did when I first left work. Being retired all of a sudden seemed to mean I was old and that made me fearful and depressed. Whatever happened to the excitement and desire to embrace life to the full when freedom first presented itself? Confusion reigned and there seemed to be no end in sight.

During this time many find themselves beset by doubts as to the wisdom of taking a planned retirement. Often, and at the most unlikely times, people can be overwhelmed with feelings of regret

about leaving work, doubt as to how smart a move
it had been and worry about what to do with all
this time to make it worthwhile, meaningful and
fulfilling. Well-honed skills seem to suddenly lack
value or significance to anyone but themselves
and the thought is devastating. Frustration, anger
and fear roil around inside and there seems to be
no escape. For some, this torment will ebb and
flow, as was Carol's experience, while for others
it might go on unabated for a period of weeks,
months or whatever time it takes to deal with the
emotional storm.

*What is your
all consuming
passion and why
does it give you
joy?*

> *The words "what have I done?" and "why did
> I leave my job?" echoed through my head time
> and again. Even though my husband and I
> were trekking in South America on an extended
> trip and I was loving every moment, I found my
> mind straying from the joy of the present and
> seeking out feelings of doubt that still lingered.
> I was on an adventure of discovery in strange
> and exotic lands, but I had not yet ventured far
> enough internally to figure out if I had taken a
> very wrong turn by giving up my career earlier
> than necessary.*

Even though we reached our retirement by very
different routes—one took a planned early retirement and the other had retirement thrust on
her by way of job elimination—the storm clouds
gathered and the storms raged. And so too, they
will for you, but you will now know that unrest is

normal and you will use the opportunity to take a good look around at everything with awareness and curiosity as you work out why your particular storm has hit.

A Blast from the Past

You're newly retired, you love the freedom and you are feeling pretty good. You've had time to catch up on all your neglected chores and tasks, get some needed rest and recuperation and do whatever takes your fancy. The possibilities are endless—visiting friends, exploring and revisiting your favourite local haunts, and luxuriating in actually having time to engage in a lengthy conversation, golf game, bike trip, or other favourite activity. That period right after leaving work is likely to be very delightful because it is so different from your previous working life schedule.

Pleasant conversations with former colleagues very often end with a comment made sincerely and with some incredulity, as to how well you look. Ah, music to the ears! On the other hand, this comment could indicate that you must have looked pretty awful while you were working!

Following fast on the heels of the previous comment comes the simple, innocuous, easy question: "And what are you doing now?" You explain about your golf, your grandkids, your reading, your gardening, your decorating, your next trip, your relaxing coffee breaks and lunches, or whatever makes up your daily routine. Life seems relaxed and good. However, as you are explaining all of this to your former colleague, you might begin to notice that while it all seems wonderful to you at the moment, it may not actually sound particularly interesting to them or on reflection, to you. Is all this activity filler or is it life?

Conversations with a former colleague can bring a torrent of emotions. It doesn't take long to realize that not much has changed at work, or perhaps everything has changed! It might sound like desperation has set in and they need your expertise, or it might all sound terribly dull, mundane and boring. It might sound like a punishment, or it might leave you wishing you were still in the fray. Either way, your reaction to information about the workplace that was such an integral and intimate part of your life can be somewhat surprising. You will likely ponder your role in that workplace and how that huge part of your life simply no longer exists.

When you're retired will you consider yourself a senior?

24/7 Passion to Boredom

There's such a build-up of positive expectation around the freedom of retirement that the tendency is to embrace it as being simply wonderful. An escape from the ordinary, a chance to do absolutely anything you want to and most importantly, when you want to. It is not difficult to succumb to those smiling images oozing out of ads promoting lifestyle choices for retirees, from vigorous vacations to reversed mortgages; appealing to your boomer expectation and desire to remain young, active, healthy and free. It has to be great—doesn't it? Yet encounters with former colleagues can put into question whether it is as wonderful as you assumed it would be or is this as good as it gets?

What happens when your passion, your hobby, your de-stressing activity, becomes ho hum? Is it really a dream come true if it happens 24/7? Maybe at first, but after a while perhaps the passion and joy that the activity provided is no longer there. That's also a bit worrying, because if you can't enjoy your passion now that you are free to indulge in it, what does that say about your life? That's what Enise asked during this stormy time.

> *I love to read; I belong to a book club. I read for pleasure and to research; my taste runs the gamut from murder mysteries and travelogues to Shakespeare and beyond. When I was working full time I would always have a book with me, and it would be my solace, providing some space for me in a busy day. If I was a little early leaving for work or some other appointment, I'd grab my latest book and stand there, coat on, shoes on, bag and stuff ready, and I'd read for a precious few minutes before heading out. Reading took me out of myself, out of my daily routine, it let me relax and gave me great satisfaction.*

Needless to say, once I became retired I took out dozens of books from the library, bought books I intended to study further, and had several on the go at the same time. The mere thought of being able to read all of these books whenever I wanted was absolutely marvellous; I could hardly wait.

I was so busy accumulating reading material that it took a while for it to dawn on me that I had several piles of books at the ready, and more on order, and yet I wasn't actually reading anything. I had time to read, I had a passion for reading, so what was wrong? I felt guilty whenever I took up a book, because I had the feeling I should be doing something.

Think about your favourite leisure time activity and imagine that you find you are no longer interested in it. This can be disconcerting to say the least. The anchor and solace in times of stress isn't there any more. You will likely find that while your activity of choice was your escape and the antidote needed to provide a balance to busy working days, as a retiree you don't need this respite in the same way. When your chosen pastime becomes your 24/7 activity and threatens to fill in the hours previously spent at work, it becomes work in itself, with all its ramifications.

Winds of Uncertainty

Now that there's time for thoughts to emerge, there is also time to consider them. And, while it's not comfortable to think about yourself as a senior and what that means, it's worthwhile considering how you arrived at your mental image of what a senior is. Likewise it is well worth considering what value your all consuming passion has to you, what prop it provided in the past, what outlet it provides to you now. Indeed is it really as enjoyable as you always told yourself it would be? and if not, why not?

If the description of your activities doesn't sound very attractive or interesting, ask yourself what it is you really want to do now. Also, make sure you go beyond all the things that you told yourself you would do, or could do, or should do.

Consider times of change in your life and what coping strategies worked well.

Now is the time to hang on and invite that storm to hit, be prepared to face it and deal with those unsettling, queasy and uncomfortable questions that come up. It's worth the work to clear the decks and take a good, unfettered look at you, your life, your habits, expectations and perceptions. You know that storms come in many styles and there's no difficulty visualizing them. How you tackle the storm will help the next time you experience the rough waters of retirement. Although it can be uncomfortable, it is nonetheless an interesting and necessary journey.

Aids to Navigation

- Be aware, look around you, notice everything, remain alert to subtle nuances and hone your senses.

- Acknowledge and honour your past life and yourself.

- It is normal to feel unsettled and at a loss, so take time to explore each inner qualm.

- Let the thoughts—good and bad—come, and remember there is time to consider them.

- View past experiences with compassion and a measure of detachment to better understand how they might be influencing you now.

- Don't suppress those unsettling feelings, instead pull them out into the light of day and take a good, hard look at what is really the cause.

CHAPTER 9

SAFE HARBOUR
Considering Your Life From Now On

When you're in a storm it makes sense to find a safe harbour as soon as possible, and it's no different for the Stormy Weather transition period after leaving work. At this stage it is good to take time to review your life, your talents, your likes and dislikes. Embrace the idea that you, yes, YOU, are actually old enough to be retired and about to enter a very exciting time of life.

It is not always easy to contemplate your future when you are not really sure who you are outside of that job title you used to have, the roles you've had in your private life, the commitments and goals you've striven for over the working years, or when those great hobbies just don't fill your days as you thought they would. Sometimes it's hard to answer when well meaning people ask, "What are you going to do?" but often it is even harder when you ask that question of yourself.

Far or Near

If you can, take a break away from the ordinary to spend time to ponder that question. Safely away mentally and/or physically from your everyday life you will start to discover just who you are now; who you were and why your life and career played out as they did. As well, what achievements and failures were yours, and why were they achievements or failures?

Take a compassionate look at yourself in old photos.

People reach their safe harbours by very different routes and use the time there in ways that best suit them. With no sense of future direction, Carol felt that her emotional turmoil seemed likely to continue unabated until a distant safe harbour beckoned.

> *My safe harbour turned out to be somewhere quite unexpected. I had long wanted to visit China, and when the opportunity unexpectedly came for me to teach there for six months, I jumped at the chance. Without a blink of an eye or discussion with my family or friends I accepted the job.*
>
> *I literally removed myself from everything familiar and safe and ventured forth on what I assumed would be an interesting interlude in what was rapidly becoming a directionless life.*

Little did I know when I made the decision to go to China that this would be an exciting journey of self-discovery and that I would have the chance to clarify who I was and what I wanted for the next few years of my life. It turned out to be a time and a space I hadn't realized I needed until I was there.

Obviously not everyone wants, or has the chance, to go to China to find a safe harbour. So, it's up to you to be creative and find time and space to devote to considering your life, looking at it from various perspectives and without input from others. You can do this on your regular long daily walks, or on a few overnight hiking or sailing trips or as you play golf, or sketch for an hour or so every day. Like many others, Enise found it hard to answer the question that was put to her most often after her job ended: "What are you going to do?"

What I needed was a break—a mental break from trying to figure out what I was going to do. I hadn't a clue and found myself assailed with questions and dawning realizations about my place in the world now as an older person. There was definitely a transition happening and at that time I simply did not know in which direction to go. I took my break by declaring "I'm taking the summer off." I was really surprised when people just shrugged and said "OK" and left it at that. That summer was the

most productive of my life. Left to my own men-
tal devices I was able to create a space in which
to explore where I was in my life, and what the
future might hold.

Whether you remove yourself by actually travel-
ling a great distance, or you make your safe harbour a figurative place, that place and that time
when you insulate yourself from decision making
about the future is something you will need.

Going Solo

Regardless of where you find your safe harbour,
this is a time when you must travel and travel
alone within yourself. Why? Because this time of
introspection is *about you* and *for you* and no one
else can do it. This is a time to reconnect with
yourself as a child or young adult, what made you
tick, what made life exciting and interesting. And
while it is a solo journey of contemplation it is also
a time to discover the self that others know. One
of the best ways to do this is to reconnect with old
school friends or childhood friends. These people knew you when you were very different from
the working adult you became. Your interaction
with them was different from that which you had
with your work colleagues, and these long ago
friends can sometimes help you again see your
childhood dreams and why you dreamed them.

*How would your
best school friend
describe you?*

This is a time to peel back the layers of memory
and investigate why you loved doing the things
you did as a child. Find those old dreams and look

at them carefully and from there create new ones. Often easier said than done, but don't be afraid to think outside of the box as to what your future might hold. Sometimes we restrict our options by attending to outmoded restrictions, imposed by the demands of our jobs, that are actually no longer applicable. Think about your hopes for the future, and do some personal brainstorming as to what you might do. Whatever it is you decide on or think about, be it relocating, going on an extended trip, studying, or taking another job, don't be afraid to ask yourself "Why?" and "Why not?"

What did you love to do when you were 8, 9 or 10 years old?

Sorting it Out

Over the years you have honed a set of skills you use whenever you need to solve a problem; what better time to put them to use than now in your safe harbour. The storm tossed seas are behind you and as you review your life, your talents and abilities, consider the things you have always wanted to do and then decide what is the essence of the specific idea that made it appealing. To find who you really are and what you would like to become, use whatever means you have at your disposal to sort through outmoded notions and the no longer applicable rules, guidelines and detritus that might be clogging up your mind. Whether it is making lists, as Enise did, or writing a journal as Carol did, find the method that works for you and use it.

This is an exciting time. This is a time of rediscovery,
a time to be truthful about your core values, a time
to fine-tune yourself, your life and your future.

Aids to Navigation

- Take time to think about your life—past, present, future.

- Review and clarify your values, desires and hopes.

- Use methods that suit you—journal, mental notes, lists, old photos.

- Think about who you are outside of the person you were at work.

- Consider what is different about this life passage from others you've been through.

- Ask yourself what you are afraid of. Whatever it is, find out about it, and understand why it bothers you.

- Think of how you can become fully engaged in life in a way that is meaningful to you and meets your values criteria.

CHAPTER 10

CHARTING YOUR OWN COURSE
Making Choices For Your Future

You are no longer looking back, but are now focusing on the future. The euphoric days and storm tossed emotions that you have experienced are better understood, and in the past. Now you're itching to move on and make choices for your future. As you begin to make decisions, you'll keep a knowledgeable weather eye open for an approaching storm, a prolonged slide into euphoria, or a mental visit to times and people past. Having invested both time and effort in considering your life thus far, you now have a handle on who you are as a person, as well as what your values truly are. You've assessed your skills and abilities, likes and dislikes, and you have a pretty good idea of the things that you love to do, and the things that you still want to accomplish. In short, you feel comfortable in the retirement mode and you're now looking forward to the future with enthusiasm.

The old structures are gone, new ones are replacing them and life is lived at a different pace. You have time to be open to ideas and possibilities that only a short time ago might have seemed out of reach or perhaps a little fantastic. You don't want to go back to the structure, routines and stresses of your old workplace, but you want to fill those long discretionary hours of retirement with something purposeful. You want to feel significant, contributory and content.

What skills do you have that are not on your resume?

Your Chart, Your Journey

As you begin to chart your own course, take time to consider the direction in which you want to go. Explore your passions and dreams, but be realistic about how you can turn them into reality. Peel back the layers to find the essence of your dreams while looking for and being open to creative ways to fulfill them. If you've always wanted to mountain climb, but now your knees have given out, find the essence of what drives your dream. Is it being up high, being alone with nature surveying distant vistas? There may be another way for you to achieve your desires without having to physically climb that mountain. Look at your hobbies and use them to sample possible directions and choices.

Researching your areas of interest will help you find out where and how it is possible to use your many skills. We all have skills that we may not have even thought of as usable in another forum. Put your expertise to work—recycle and refurbish your skills to benefit yourself and others. Now is the time to step outside of the limitations that might have been imposed upon you when you were working, and to make some changes.

So Many Choices

As you move forward and begin to chart your own course, consider your own criteria for success. Ask yourself if making money is the only reason to do a job. What rewards might there be in a volunteer position? Starting a business is a possibility—Stats Can tells us the fastest growing group of successful entrepreneurs are retired people. Given that by 2011 more than 20% of our population will be 61 or older and there will be fewer young people entering the workplace, there will be many new, diversified opportunities.

What is your definition of a volunteer?

There are many opportunities for volunteers in areas that might interest you or that you feel passionate about. Volunteering can offer you an opportunity to use your unique skills and experience, and give you a whole new perspective. It is worth considering how you view volunteer positions. Some people shy away from volunteering because "there's no money in it" even when they may not actually be in need of money. By making such a decision, people chance depriving themselves of enriching experiences due to outmoded perceptions. And because there are so many capable people approaching retirement, there might be competition in getting a volunteer position that particularly appeals to you. Start now if you want to work with a particular organization or group, get involved in a small way so that you can expand your involvement later.

All people, when charting their own courses, go about it in a way that suits their needs, and we were no different. Our experience was by no means unique and it serves as an example of what you might go through as you begin this final phase. Here's how we tackled charting our own courses into retirement.

Remember, most people take more time planning their annual vacation than they do their retirement.

Our Chart, Our Journey

We have been friends for a number of years, although we had never worked together or spent lengthy periods of time in each other's company. We shared many similar interests—sailing, travel and reading are a few. Before we really understood what we were experiencing during those early days of our retirements, we'd meet every so often to discuss where we were in our lives, and what we were thinking, and how we were feeling. Compelled by our own inquisitiveness and the need for information, we began to read and research retirement. Being people who like to organize and provide others with information, it was a natural evolution for us to decide we had to get the information "out there." When we began to chart our own courses we didn't take the easy way out, but instead stretched ourselves as individuals, and channeled our abilities. We acquired new skills and honed existing ones by tackling sophisticated electronic equipment, working with new software, creating useable materials, interviewing people, and becoming the subject of interviews ourselves. All this gave each of us a sense of achievement and focus, something we both knew we wanted and needed. Our current incarnations, as workshop presenters and authors, is the outcome of our search to chart courses that allowed us to be actively engaged in our retirements, and the best thing is, it doesn't feel like work!

There's a whole world of opportunities out there, but you can't expect the right thing for you to just drop into your lap. You'll need to do some research, read and ask a lot of questions. Whatever you decide, don't be afraid to explore, to experiment and if necessary, to change until you find that special something you've been looking for to give purpose and direction to your new life. It could be anything from paid employment, travel, studying, writing, reading, gardening, a new career, volunteering, entering politics, even teaching. But, whatever it is, remember that in today's world *your* retirement is whatever *you* want it to be!

Aids to Navigation

- Find the essence of your dreams and be creative in finding ways to fulfill them.

- Research areas of interest to find out how you can use your skills in other ways.

- Take time to really consider the direction in which you wish to travel.

- Be honest with yourself about your capabilities.

- Take your proven past experience and knowledge and use them as an embarkation point.

- Be prepared to scrap an idea if it isn't working—it's a positive not a negative step.

CHAPTER 11

YOUR CREW AND YOU
Relationships Before and After

While not a phase in the retirement continuum, this chapter is essential when planning for your retirement. Who are the people in your personal network and what does your retirement mean to them? Whether they are family, friends, acquaintances, colleagues, distant relatives, neighbours, service providers, or club members, many people will be affected by your retirement. You'll likely receive comments, suggestions, observations, words of wisdom, helpful hints, words of warning and advice not necessarily needed or wanted.

The intent of the following list is not to categorize or label people, nor be a definitive list of relationships that you might have. It does, however, provide an overview of some of the considerations that others with whom you interact might bring to your retirement plans, and poses a few questions you might not have asked yourself.

Spouse/Partner

Do you know what your partner's vision of retirement is or what she/he wants to do when retired?

Does your partner know your vision of retirement?

The person with whom you share most of your life is likely as much in the dark about your retirement as you are, and vice versa. In the business of the working day, this topic is usually discussed in terms of financial arrangements and a vague wish list of things that might come to pass. Or it could be that one person has very definite ideas about how to spend those retirement years, and the other hasn't really absorbed the implications, or bought in to the vision.

For Enise, whose retirement landed on her unexpectedly, it was quickly obvious some discussion with her husband had been lacking.

> *My husband had never known me as anyone other than a full time post-secondary Education Administrator with adult children who had their own careers. So when my job unexpectedly ended he had trouble deciding whether I was unemployed or retired. I was at home, but*

*he hardly dared to conceive of me as a stereo-
typical housewife because the habits he thought
were required for this designation were not those
I displayed with great enthusiasm. I had gone
from the yuppie he first met to a retiree/senior in
one fell swoop, so was I teetering on the brink
of old age and about to adopt a way of being
that was reminiscent of his grandparents' generation? As a consequence, he was very helpful
in bringing potential job opportunities to my
attention. Simultaneously, I wasn't so sure I
wanted to go back to the type of work I'd left. I
had embarked on the Stormy Seas of fairly uncomfortable self-exploration. Truth of the matter was, neither of us had a clue what the other
really thought of our respective retirements, and
now the topic was staring us in the face. Needless to say it was a bit of a shake-up.*

Already at Home

If one person is already at home when the other retires, then some adjustment in simple daily
routines is inevitable. The newly retired person
might not enjoy the other's routines or how social and other activities now impose a structure
on their days, just as being in the workplace used
to. When the new retiree tries to fit into this new
structure and way of living, the process may become very trying indeed to both people. One not
quite fitting in and perhaps wanting to change
things, the other maybe resenting being "joined
at the hip" or alternatively, the total indifference

of the newly retired person to things on the home front. Long into retirement himself, Carol's husband was pleased by her decision to take early retirement and had many ideas and plans for the time they could now spend together.

> *When my husband semi-officially retired, I had close to 15 more years ahead of me in the workplace before I would be taking my planned early retirement. Like many women, I found my professional stride later in life and wanted to continue my teaching career even though my husband, who is older, was anxious for me to join him in retirement. However, whenever we could we traveled, renovated houses, sailed, enjoyed social activities together and always looked forward to more extensive involvement when I actually retired. When the great day arrived, life followed the pattern we, and most particularly I, assumed it would. My husband and I enjoyed doing things together; however, as time passed I found being together 24/7 began to be too much of a good thing. Forging a separate, yet together, schedule took ingenuity, but most of all patience, something that wasn't always apparent during those early days.*

Retiring Together

Perhaps you are typical of many who have never spent extended periods of time together other than on vacation. You've raised children, studied, worked, played and generally moved from being young adults to retirees—your lives have been parallel and connected but not identical. Now suddenly, you can spend all your daily life with your partner, not just while on holiday and not for a short period of time.

Jobs impose structures on our time, but when we're retired they are gone. Work had influenced all the essential minutiae of daily life—when you took time off, when you got up or went to bed, what you had for breakfast, and whether or not you had dinner at home, what kind of transportation you used, and so on. In retirement you can create your own living structure which is both wonderful and challenging.

Are there any cultural considerations that might influence how you spend your retirement?

Consider something relatively simple like when you'll take your morning coffee or tea. Did one person habitually wait until reaching the workplace before the first cup of the day? Does the other reach for the kettle immediately upon leaving the bed? Maybe you left for work at different times and don't even know what your partner's habits are in this regard because it didn't matter much. Perhaps you will now want to stay in bed longer, or wish to sit outside and enjoy the beverage together while contemplating the day, or maybe you want to linger over the newspaper in solitude. Something relatively simple can become a focus for too much discussion once we are left to recreate our own ways of living.

You have time to do things together, but you also need time to explore life on your own, and it takes goodwill and much effort to move forward into retirement, together.

Friends

Over the years we share and support our work colleagues through life's challenges and joys. Outside of the workplace, do you consider these former colleagues your friends? Ask yourself what you have in common. Consider whether these were friendships of convenience because you were all in the same boat, so to speak, or deep enduring connections for life. If you've invested a lot of time and energy into work based relationships, you might find yourself somewhat bereft because your position is now changed.

If there are health challenges, how will you find the essence of what it is you want to do so you can adapt to circumstances?

Being retired is a great time to reconnect with old friends, and the Internet is a useful tool in finding where they might be. Reminiscing about the times you spent together as youngsters helps you discover many forgotten parts of yourself because friends can offer you glimpses of how and why they remember you.

Where do former colleagues who are also friends fit in with old friends or those acquired through shared activities and newly developed interests? It no longer matters what you did at work, what your position was or where you were in the real or imagined hierarchy, because now your friends will be made because of who you are. It's very freeing to engage in all manner of activities and interests without applying limitations based on who you are in a workplace. As a boater once said, "When you're heading for the dock and the wind is blowing, the water is rough and you're tense at the wheel but there are people there to catch the lines, it doesn't matter a darn what they did for a living, they are heroes now!"

Sitter on Call

In retirement, what will be your role with regard to support for your parents, children, or grandchildren?

Do your children think of your retirement as unlimited access to free babysitting? Or are they dreading your increased presence in their lives when you retire? Either way, it's worthwhile finding out ahead of time what ideas your children have about your retirement, and consider how you feel about your role as grandparent and parent.

Caregiver

As the "sandwich generation"—people sandwiched between aging parents who need care and their own children—we all know that obligations to aging parents might impinge on retirement dreams. It is important to take the time to investigate the various possibilities, options and services available to your parents well before any might be needed. Be warned though, in delving into services and possibilities for the aged it becomes increasingly clear that you are not so far off heading down that same road. This telescoping of the years ahead can be very unsettling for those who are just coming to terms with the fact that in some circles they are tagged as seniors.

There are many relationship issues for those contemplating retirement. Health concerns and different cultural attitudes towards retirement are just two of the myriad problems that can impinge on an individual or a couple's retirement. It is wise to consider all issues, no matter the particular situation, as objectively, honestly and positively as you can.

Aids to Navigation

- Consider how others might view your retirement.

- Define friendship, then consider who are your friends, acquaintances, companions.

- Find out the retirement dreams of those who are closest to you.

- "Senior" can apply to you and your parents—remind yourself there is a generation of difference.

- Be conscious that the structure of your life when you are working will change when you retire.

- Know that some habits that formed part of your daily structure may no longer be as important or significant as you once thought.

CHAPTER 12

BON VOYAGE
En Route to the Rest of Your Life

This is without doubt the best of possible times in which a soon-to-be retired person can live. Not only are people in their 50s and 60s healthier and more active than ever before, but they are armed with an insatiable curiosity and a desire to experience life to the fullest for some time to come. As the old stereotypical perceptions of seniors and older people give way to more realistic images reflective of how we are today, our reticence to embrace this stage of life will disappear.

With a wealth of life experience, good ideas, myriad skills, proven abilities to change things for the better and with a broader perspective and some compassion garnered over the years, this generation now has the chance to look at life from a different vantage point and see an interesting and fulfilling future ahead. Make the most of what you have to offer and make the most of your life from now on, for, as Mark Twain says:

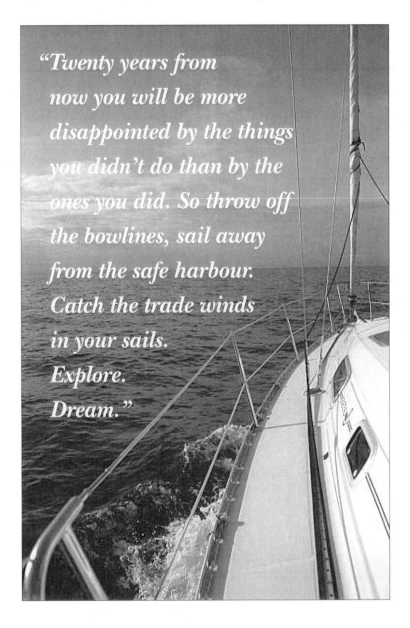

"Twenty years from now you will be more disappointed by the things you didn't do than by the ones you did. So throw off the bowlines, sail away from the safe harbour. Catch the trade winds in your sails. Explore. Dream."

CHAPTER 13

MORE AIDS TO NAVIGATION
Other Helpful Resources

Useful Books

Now that you've read this book you might want to further delve into the topic of retirement and life after finishing work. Here are some of the books we found to be helpful and interesting and which will provide you with more information on the wide-ranging topic of retirement.

The Healing Journey Through Retirement
Phil Rich, Dorothy Madway Sampson, Dale S. Fetherling
John Wiley & Sons Inc., Canada/USA, 2000
ISBN 0-471-32693-3

If you'd like a gentle approach to understanding and working through the transition from work to retirement, this is the book for you. Along with several work pages, which you can choose to complete or simply contemplate, this book brings a very thorough look at the experiences one might expect to have upon entering retirement. The reader is encouraged to look beyond the obvious, and beyond the answers to the questions to find out why the answers were given, upon what they are based and where they come from. This is an encouraging book which helps readers look inside themselves while at the same time journey down all the pathways of life with open eyes to find a new sense of understanding upon which to base future plans.

It's Only Too Late If You Don't Start Now – How to Create Your Second Life At Any Age
Barbara Sher
Dell Trade Paperback, NY, 1999
ISBN 0-440-50718-9

In this book the glass is definitely half full and not half empty at mid-life. Although the age of 40 is mentioned throughout the book, it applies equally for 50, 60 and onward. Viewing the stages of human life from nature's vantage point certainly helps make clear that all the twists, turns and hands of fate we've been dealt are by and large unavoidable. In other words, it is all normal. If you are poised on the brink of mid-life, this book will turn around any notions of despair about being on the slippery slope to declining old age ending in the arms of the grim reaper. A heartening read mainly because life's passages and nature's influences on our lives is explained in encouraging and understandable ways.

Don't Retire, Rewire! 5 Steps to Fulfilling Work That Fuels Your Passion, Suits Your Personality, or Fills your Pocket
Jeri Sedlar, Rick Miners
Alpha Books and Pearson Education,
Indianapolis, IN, 2003.
ISBN 0-02-864228-7

If you're considering another career, job or earning opportunity after retirement, then this book will help you get going. Examples of others who have chosen to move in another direction to earn money, enhance and broaden their lives are given. But most important are the tools to help you discover how to "rewire" and start on another earning pathway; these include learning about yourself and what drives you, what you're good at, and what you love to do. Included are tips and ideas about getting your new life up and running. This book is not just about finding another full-time job; it is more about finding an occupation (which could be paid or unpaid) that fits your lifestyle, your values and your schedule.

The Healthy Boomer: A No-Nonsense Midlife Health Guide for Women and Men
Peggy Edwards, Miroslava Lhotsky, M.D., Judy Turner, Ph.D

McClelland & Stewart, Inc., Toronto, 1999
ISBN 0-7710-3050-9

This book can be helpful for someone in the turmoil of mid-life and concerned about health issues. It helps to educate and clarify some of the physical changes that occur at mid-life. As the title says, this is a no-nonsense guide and because the information is given in an approachable style it goes a long way to making anyone experiencing the challenges of mid-life feel normal. Armed with solid, pertinent information, this book helps in the decision making that is an important part of this time in life. Often heard on radio interviews as timely issues of interest to the boomer generation emerge, the authors build on the basic practical advice given in this book. This book will help men, women and couples, as the back cover says, "on the journey from mid-life turbulence to mid-life mastery."

Future Perfect: Retirement Strategies for Productive People
David Bond and Diane Bond
Douglas & McIntyre, Vancouver/Toronto, 2002
ISBN 1-55054-957-X

Definitely one of the most upbeat books about people and retirement. The book's positive tone and use of real people who've made the adjustment from a productive career to an engaged and fulfilling retirement is both enlightening and stimulating. The ideas and thoughts of the people included in the book showed, that with planning, retirement can be the best career a person can have. Although some of the people profiled are Canadian household names, the book is not about the rich and famous, but rather a down-to- earth, engaging look at people who have made a major transition in their lives. *Future Perfect* is a perfect book to read when contemplating retirement. It is easy to read, thought provoking and positive to the point that the reader can't help but be energized.

Retirement Guide for Canadians: An overall plan for a comfortable future
Henry S. Hunnisett
Self-Counsel Press, Canada and USA, 1993
ISBN 0-88908-866-7

Originally published thirty years ago, the information in this book is nevertheless definitely appropriate for today and extremely useful. Beginning with the question "Are you ready to retire?" this book looks at all aspects of retirement. Based on the author's own experiences, the book covers the psychological, emotional and financial areas that should be carefully considered by anyone contemplating retirement. It is a manual for retirement and full of good solid advice, given in clear, straightforward, easily understood language. If you want to cover all your bases in one book, this little gem is it!

*For Better or For Worse But Not For Lunch: Making
Marriage Work in Retirement*
Sara Yogev
Contemporary Books, New York, 2002
ISBN 0-8092-9720-5

Using a take off on the Lynn Johnson comic strip
or the traditional marriage vow as part of its title,
this book deals with the rather difficult topic of
relationships in retirement gently but firmly. Because today so much emphasis is put on the financial aspects of retirement, most people do not
think about how unstructured time, loss of one's
professional identity combined with constant to-
getherness will affect the singular most important
relationship in their lives. This book, written by a
psychologist with years of experience in counsel-
ling couples, provides exercises, techniques and
guidelines to help people prepare and weather
any storms that might come their way as they
embark on this major transition. This is not a
heavy-handed tome. The subject is covered with
humour and is written in jargon free language.
If you're both retiring, or one is already retired,
or one partner is retiring and the other isn't, this
book is worth reading and sharing.

Worthwhile Websites

Because websites frequently change, we have included only a few that might be of interest as you contemplate the years ahead.

www.goodtimes.ca

The website for *Good Times Magazine* mirrors the excellent magazine for those who are in the 50+ age group.

www.50plus.com and www.carp.ca

These websites for the Canadian Association of Retired Persons provide good information about a wide variety of issues of interest to people who are retired.

www.seniors.gc.ca

Government of Canada site dedicated to providing information and services available to seniors.

http://www.retirementplanners.ca/

Canadian Association of Pre-Retirement Planners CAPP is a National Organization. It consists of provincial or regional chapters and individuals dedicated to the development and delivery of retirement planning programs. It is governed by a Board of Directors composed of chapter representatives. A variety of pre-retirement planning services from financial to lifestyle and transition are offered by members, many of whom are accredited Professional Retirement Planners.

www.elderhostel.org
Elderhostel
This site has a link to the Canadian organization. Adventures in Lifelong Learning are offered by way of a variety of innovative, exciting and unusual travel opportunities.

www.caa.ca
The Canadian Automobile Association
An excellent source to find out about driving, travel, maps, insurance, weather and a whole lot more to do with travel.

www.ceso-saco.com
Canadian Executive Service Organization (CESO)
Just one of the many services in which it is involved CESO engages Canadians as Volunteer Advisers (VAs) to share their business, technical and/or professional expertise.

www.CUSO.org
CUSO volunteer cooperants are skilled professionals who donate their expertise for up to two years to participate in a CUSO program overseas. There are volunteer opportunities within Canada, and a variety of programs in which to become involved.

Log It
Your Thoughts and Ideas

_____

_____

_____

_____

_____

_____

_____

_____

_____

_____

_____

_____

_____

_____

_____

_____

_____

_____

_____

_____

_____

_____

_____

_____

_____

_____